READING POWER

Nature's Greatest Hits

Angel Falls
World's Highest Waterfall

Joanne Mattern

The Rosen Publishing Group's
PowerKids Press™
New York

Published in 2002 by The Rosen Publishing Group, Inc.
29 East 21st Street, New York, NY 10010

First Edition

Book Design: Michael DeLisio

Photo Credits: Cover, pp. 8–9, 20–21 © Yann Arthus-Bertrand/Corbis; pp. 5, 14–15 © Jay Dickman/Corbis; p. 7 © Richard List/Corbis; pp. 9 (inset), 19 © Pablo Corral V/Corbis; pp. 10–11, 17 © Chris Rainier/Corbis; p. 13 © Bettmann/Corbis.

Mattern, Joanne, 1963–
Angel Falls: world's highest waterfall / Joanne Mattern.
   p. cm. — (Nature's greatest hits)
Includes bibliographical references (p.   ).
ISBN 0-8239-6016-1 (lib. bdg.)
1. Angel Falls (Venezuela)—Juvenile literature. [1. Angel Falls (Venezuela)] I. Title. II. Series.
GB1480.A54 M38 2001
551.48'4'098763—dc21

                                        2001000271

Manufactured in the United States of America

Contents

World's Highest Waterfall

Angel Falls is the highest waterfall in the world. It is 3,212 feet high. It is more than 16 times higher than Niagara Falls in New York.

The World's Highest Waterfalls

Name	Location	Height
Angel Falls	Venezuela	3,212 feet
Tugela Falls	South Africa	2,800 feet
Utigard Falls	Norway	2,625 feet
Monge Falls	Norway	2,540 feet
Mutarazi Falls	Japan	2,499 feet

In one part of Angel Falls, the water drops 2,648 feet without a break. The water of Angel Falls drops into a river.

2,648 feet

Location

Angel Falls is in Venezuela, a country in South America. The area around Angel Falls has many large mesas, or flat-topped hills. Rain forests and flatlands cover the mesas.

Venezuela

South America

The water of Angel Falls drops from a mesa called Devil Mountain. The rocks of this mesa are some of the oldest rocks on Earth.

IT'S A FACT: The rocks of Devil Mountain are made of sandstone and are billions of years old!

11

History

Ancient people thought that Angel Falls was a sacred, or holy, place. They believed that going to the base of Angel Falls brought bad luck.

Base

13

In the 1930s, an American pilot from Missouri, James Angel, landed his plane near the waterfall. He was the first person from outside of Venezuela to see it. The waterfall was named for him.

IT'S A FACT: James Angel's plane is now on display at an airport in Venezuela.

James Angel

Getting There

A thick jungle surrounds Angel Falls. It is a very hard place to visit. Some people get there by flying in small planes or helicopters.

This view of Angel Falls is from an airplane.

Other visitors take canoes up the river. Then they can hike to the base of Angel Falls.

IT'S A FACT: In 1971, it took three climbers ten days to climb from the bottom of Angel Falls to the top.

Visitors to Angel Falls say that it is a great sight to see. They all talk about its large size and the loud sound of the falling waters. Visitors will always remember Angel Falls, the world's highest waterfall.

Glossary

ancient (**ayn**-shuhnt) having lived a very long time ago; very old

base (**bays**) the bottom of something

flatlands (**flat**-landz) lands without hills or valleys

mesa (**may**-suh) a flat-topped hill

rain forests (**rayn for**-ihsts) thick evergreen forests in tropical regions with a yearly rainfall of 100 inches or more

sacred (**say**-krihd) highly respected and thought to be very important

sandstone (**sand**-stohn) a kind of rock that is formed mostly from sand

waterfall (**waw**-tuhr-fawl) a natural stream of water that falls from a high place

Resources

Books

The Wonder of a Waterfall
by Allan Fowler
Children's Press (1999)

Waterfalls: Forces of Nature Series
by Andrew Donnelly
The Child's World, Inc. (1998)

Web Site

Extreme Science
http://www.extremescience.com/Hfallspage.htm

Index

Word Count: 289

Note to Librarians, Teachers, and Parents

If reading is a challenge, Reading Power is a solution! Reading Power is perfect for readers who want high-interest subject matter at an accessible reading level. These fact-filled, photo-illustrated books are designed for readers who want straightforward vocabulary, engaging topics, and a manageable reading experience. With clear picture/text correspondence, leveled Reading Power books put the reader in charge. Now readers have the power to get the information they want and the skills they need in a user-friendly format.